# RENEWABLE ENERGY RESOURCES

## UNDERSTANDING GLOBAL ISSUES

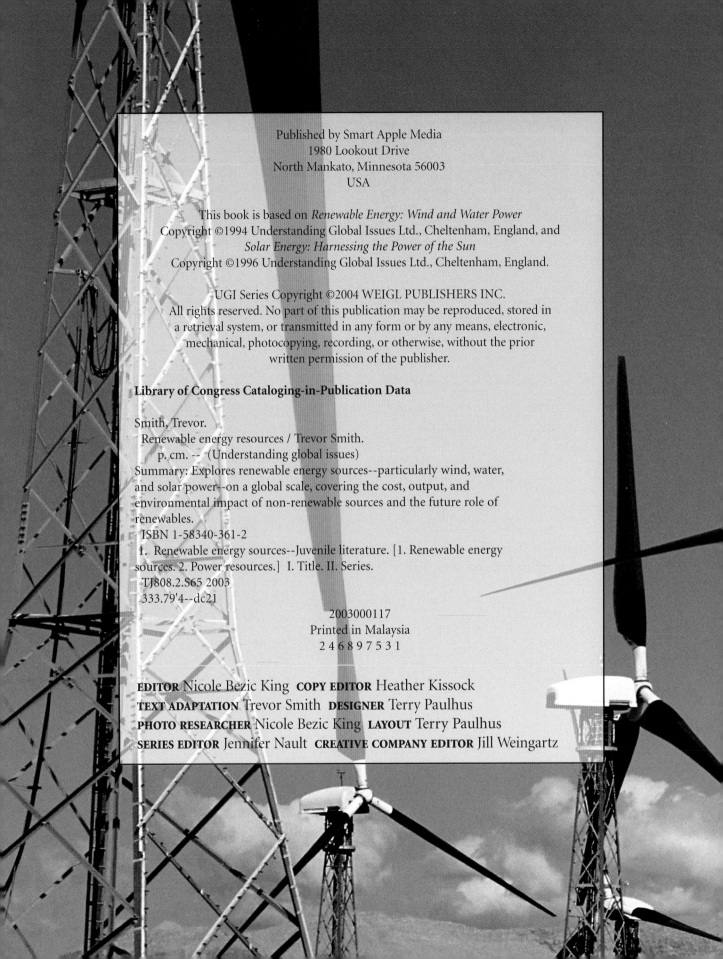

Published by Smart Apple Media
1980 Lookout Drive
North Mankato, Minnesota 56003
USA

This book is based on *Renewable Energy: Wind and Water Power*
Copyright ©1994 Understanding Global Issues Ltd., Cheltenham, England, and
*Solar Energy: Harnessing the Power of the Sun*
Copyright ©1996 Understanding Global Issues Ltd., Cheltenham, England.

UGI Series Copyright ©2004 WEIGL PUBLISHERS INC.

**Library of Congress Cataloging-in-Publication Data**

Smith, Trevor.
  Renewable energy resources / Trevor Smith.
    p. cm. -- (Understanding global issues)
Summary: Explores renewable energy sources--particularly wind, water,
and solar power--on a global scale, covering the cost, output, and
environmental impact of non-renewable sources and the future role of
renewables.
  ISBN 1-58340-361-2
  1. Renewable energy sources--Juvenile literature. [1. Renewable energy
sources. 2. Power resources.]  I. Title. II. Series.
  TJ808.2.S65 2003
  333.79'4--dc21

2003000117
Printed in Malaysia
2 4 6 8 9 7 5 3 1

**EDITOR** Nicole Bezic King  **COPY EDITOR** Heather Kissock
**TEXT ADAPTATION** Trevor Smith  **DESIGNER** Terry Paulhus
**PHOTO RESEARCHER** Nicole Bezic King  **LAYOUT** Terry Paulhus
**SERIES EDITOR** Jennifer Nault  **CREATIVE COMPANY EDITOR** Jill Weingartz

# Contents

# Introduction

The world runs on energy. Imagine if everything stopped at once—if there was no electricity and no gas. Imagine not being able to travel or modify the temperature of your home. Imagine how quiet it would be with no vehicles, and think how clean the air would be. About 85 percent of the world's energy comes from sources that are finite, meaning they will eventually run out.

**Fossil fuels** such as oil, coal, and natural gas will not last forever. Many predictions have oil running short in 40 years. Coal may last a few decades longer, anywhere from 75 to 200 years. With rising populations and increased development in the **developing world**, the world will eventually have to turn elsewhere for power.

**Renewable energy** resources, such as water, wind, and solar power, are those resources that do not run out. Better still, unlike fossil fuels, they emit almost no carbon dioxide. Society relied on renewable resources, such as wood and the sun's warmth and light, until the **Industrial Revolution**. At this time, coal came into favor. Cheap, efficient oil and gas eventually came into widespread use during the 20th century, replacing renewable resources in

all but the poorest of nations. The recent reliance on fossil fuels has had serious consequences, however. Not only will fossil fuels run out sometime in the not-too-distant future, they also have a major impact on the environment and atmosphere, releasing emissions that most scientists believe contribute to global warming.

Solar and wind power fall into the "other" category of world power usage. Together, they account for less than one percent of the world's energy. Hydroelectric power is the only renewable resource in major use worldwide. Nearly 20 percent of worldwide electricity production comes from hydropower, and in the United States, it supplies approximately 10 percent of

*Fossil fuels such as oil, coal, and natural gas will not last forever.*

the nation's electricity. There is boundless energy in the movement of water. By simply placing a **turbine** in the path of water, electricity can be generated and even stored. Even the ocean tides can be used to supply power. Although hydroelectric power does cause some environmental concerns, it adds almost no carbon dioxide ($CO_2$) or other pollutants to the atmosphere.

Though solar and wind power make up a small proportion of world energy, wind power is a fast-growing industry. At the best sites in the world, wind energy is already competing with fossil fuels in national power grids. While wind use may be insignificant now, groups such as the European Wind Energy Association and Greenpeace suggest that, providing the political will exists, wind could provide 12 percent of the world's electricity by 2020. Already, wind power is able to meet the electricity needs of about 35 million people, or 14 million households, worldwide. Wind energy used on a **commercial** scale, for grid-connected electricity, has been on the increase, especially in the U.S. and northern Europe. With a global growth rate of 15 to 20 percent per year throughout the 1990s, wind may yet prove to be a powerful weapon in the fight against global warming. It may also avert any energy crisis that will inevitably occur if our dependence on fossil fuels is to continue.

The large-scale harnessing of solar energy has long been a dream of environmentalists, but in practice, it has generally proven to be a letdown. The sun delivers, for free, 10,000 times the energy humans require. However, converting it into useable power is difficult. That is why solar energy currently accounts for only 0.04 percent of worldwide energy production. The technologies of the past have not been able to convert enough sunlight into electricity or heat to make solar energy economical on a large scale. This could change soon. In Israel, more than 80 percent of homes have solar hot water. Through the miracle of **photovoltaics** (PV), sunlight can be turned directly into electricity. Used to power lighthouses, buoys, and road-sign indicators, solar power may yet fulfill the dream of cheap, clean power.

▨ **Energy is the foundation upon which thriving economies are built.**

# Large-Scale Hydropower

ydroelectric power is the only form of renewable energy that has been able to compete on a large scale with fossil fuels. As it is, almost

**The Grand Coulee Dam in Washington is the largest producer of hydroelectric power in the United States.**

20 percent of global electricity production comes from hydropower, and most of that comes from large dams. Dams are structures that block and control the flow of a major river. Water is let through the dam and turns massive turbines. These turbines are connected to generators. As the turbines

rotate, the generators produce electricity that is then fed into the power grid for use by consumers. The water remains unchanged and continues on its way. Rainy mountain valleys can also be dammed. Norway, for instance, has many fast-flowing mountain rivers and three of the highest waterfalls in the world.

This allows Norway to obtain almost all of its electricity from hydropower. Canada and the United States also have major hydropower systems. However, over time, these **developed countries** will see less expansion of the hydro industry. This is because countries in the developed world have already turned most of their promising sites into power stations. North America, for instance, has already developed three-quarters of its hydro potential.

Most dams are built not to provide power, but to control flooding and provide water for domestic and industrial use. The

> ### *Most dams are built to control flooding and provide water.*

massive Three Gorges project, in which the Yangtze River in China is to be dammed, is aimed at protecting the people who live along the banks of Asia's longest river. In years of heavy rain, the river normally rises, and those living closest to it face losing their homes and even their lives. The Three Gorges Dam is expected to control the level of the river and keep it from swelling in wet years. But this dam has tremendous power potential as well. A power plant located there will produce more than 18,000 megawatts, enough to satisfy the energy demands of users throughout central China.

## PUMPED STORAGE

Hydroelectric power can be stored for future use as "pumped storage." In times of low power usage, power produced at a pumped storage hydro plant can be used to reverse turbines and pump water up into an upper **reservoir**. When demand becomes high again, the water can be released, falling down to turn turbines and produce electricity. The same can be done with a wind farm, where wind turbines turn whether or not there is a demand for electricity.

**The Grand Coulee Dam's 28 generators produce enough electricity to make it the main source of electric power in America's Northwest.**

This must have been a major factor in the government's decision to proceed with the controversial plan.

About two-thirds of the world's potential for hydropower remains untapped. It is estimated that hydropower will grow 2.5 to 3 percent per year over the next few decades. It will remain the leader in renewable energy for many decades. Such growth will likely take place in the developing world. Countries using dams will be able to grow faster economically and enjoy a higher standard of living while producing energy without creating carbon dioxide or other greenhouse gases.

Hydroelectric power does not come without problems. In fact, large-scale hydro projects often create their own brand of social and environmental ills. People often build homes near rivers because they are a source of food and water. A dam creates a large reservoir behind it, so what was once a river becomes a lake behind the dam. While the dam may save houses downstream, it may mean that thousands more upstream will be displaced before it is

▓ **According to government officials, the Three Gorges Dam may eventually provide 11 percent of China's electricity.**

completed. Populations all over the world have been displaced as a result of the construction of large-scale dams.

## THE THREE GORGES DAM

The Three Gorges Dam has been a controversial project from its beginning. Construction on the dam began in 1994, with a scheduled completion date of 2016. When complete, this dam will be the largest in the world, at 1.3 miles (2.1 km) long and 610 feet (186 m) high. As well, a reservoir approximately 400 miles (650 km) long will be created. This reservoir will cover 150,000 acres (60,700 ha) of land with water. Close to two million people will have to be relocated, and 160 towns, 16 archaeological sites, and 8,000 cultural sites will all be underwater.

Those who support the dam believe it will save lives by preventing future floods. This is an area where more than 250,000 lives were lost to flooding between 1930 and 1935. Supporters also believe that the power generated by the dam will bring development and increased living standards to the region. Many also believe that this will reduce China's dependence on coal and thus decrease air pollution. Those who oppose the building of the dam feel that the high cost will ruin the Chinese economy. They are also worried about the environmental impact of the dam. They believe that the loss of cultural relics and historical sites, as well as the effect of forced relocation on a large number of people, is not worth any positive impact the dam may bring.

Dams can also cause major damage to **ecosystems** in the area. Plants that grow along a river cannot survive if they have been covered by a dam-made lake, though some species may begin to grow along the "new" shoreline. Many animals cannot adapt well either. For example, fish migrate in regular patterns, and these patterns are negatively impacted by dams.

The Snake River Dams, near Seattle, Washington, are an example of how dams can affect the environment. In the late 1990s, salmon populations were decreasing due to the dams. The dams reduced the speed of the river, allowing it to be choked by weeds and algae. The salmon, which require cold, fast-flowing water, have been severely reduced in number. There is little doubt that salmon stocks would be helped by removing the dams. Still, with power in high demand in Oregon and continued power outages in California, there is a lot of pressure to maintain the Snake River Dams.

Extensive environmental assessments must be carried out before a dam can be built. There must be proof that damage to local ecosystems will be minimal. Still, there are times when, in the interest of economic and social needs, potential damage may be overlooked.

Another drawback to large-scale dams is the huge cost involved. Turbines are expensive, as are the resources and technologies used to build a dam. This has often prevented developing countries from constructing dams. However, once a dam is operational, running costs are very low. The fuel—water—is free. Dams are also highly efficient. Whereas a typical fossil fuel plant is able to convert about 50 percent of available energy into electricity, large-scale hydropower plants are able to convert significantly more—90 percent. These factors increase their popularity with many governments, particularly those in the developing world. Dams do not contribute to global warming. They are also the most logical environmental choice for now. Perhaps technologies in the future will make hydropower as efficient as it is today, but without harmful environmental effects. Alternatively, new and improved technologies may replace hydropower with truly **green** forms of energy, such as solar or wind power.

## EVERYTHING UNDER THE SUN

Strictly speaking, all forms of energy, except for tidal, **geothermal**, and nuclear energy, are solar. Wind is created when the sun heats air masses. Hydropower derives from the sun-powered cycle of evaporation and rain. Photosynthesis allows the sun's energy to be stored in the **organic** matter used to produce **bioenergy**, and the sun affects and creates marine currents. Even fossil fuels come from solar energy, which was stored in the plants and animals that formed coal, oil, and natural gas millions of years ago.

## KEY CONCEPTS

**Environmental assessment** Before a major project such as a power plant or dam can be constructed, its effects on land, air, water, and wildlife in the area must be determined. An environmental assessment is a decision-making tool used by an agency or company. It is not generally available to the public. It may also outline positive steps, such as the introduction of diversion systems, that can be taken to avert negative impacts.

**Global warming** The average temperature on Earth is on the rise. Although this may be due in part to natural variation, many scientists believe the increase is largely a result of industrial processes that are ultimately leading to changes in climate. When climate changes, patterns of rainfall and sea levels also change. Climate change can result in a range of negative impacts on plants and animals.

**Greenhouse gases** The six main greenhouse gases are carbon dioxide, hydroflurocarbons, nitrous oxide, sulfur haxafluoride, methane, and perfluorocarbons. Energy radiated by the sun travels to Earth and warms the surface. Some of this energy becomes trapped in the atmosphere by gases such as carbon dioxide. As a result, the lower portion of Earth's atmosphere experiences a rise in temperature. This is referred to as the "greenhouse effect." Most

Salmon and trout are among the animals most commonly affected by large-scale dams. Insects, young fish, and many other organisms—food sources for other wildlife—are also often negatively impacted.

scientists acknowledge the greenhouse effect, but there is much debate about the causes and effects.

**Kilowatt, megawatt, gigawatt**
Electricity is measured in watts. A watt is simply a measure of power over time. One kilowatt (kW) is equal to 1,000 watts, or the amount of energy needed to light ten 100-watt lightbulbs. One megawatt (MW) is one million watts, or 1,000 kilowatts.

A gigawatt (GW) is the equivalent of one billion watts, or 1,000 megawatts. A terawatt (TW) is equal to 1,000 gigawatts.

**Power grid** A power grid is a network of power lines that connects power plants to consumers. Although the grid is broken down into about 150 subsections in North America, it is a single energy-distributing machine. It stretches 3,000 miles (5,000 km) from north to south

and 3,000 miles from east to west, covering the entire U.S. and much of Canada. Each substation acts as a crossroad on the grid. These substations enable power companies to buy and sell power from each other as well as monitor their energy supply on a more local basis. Electricity for one location can come from anywhere in the country.

# Small-Scale Hydro and Ocean Power

Only four percent of all the electricity produced from hydropower comes from small-scale projects. These smaller projects are important for many reasons. They are more environmentally friendly than large-scale dams. For example, small-scale hydro is often used on small, swift rivers and does not truly dam them. Small-scale hydro projects have a long life, with turbines and generators lasting 20 to 30 years, and the concrete works that sometimes support them lasting 100 years or more. Once in place, small-scale projects are inexpensive to maintain. They are often built on existing structures. Also, continual improvements in technology can make small-scale projects more efficient than they already are.

Small hydropower systems are divided into three classes of facilities. Micro facilities produce less than 100 kilowatts. Mini facilities produce between 100

**The amount of energy that can be generated from falling water is affected by the volume of water and the vertical distance it drops. The greater the volume and distance, the larger the amount of energy produced.**

kilowatts and 1 megawatt, and facilities that produce between 1 and 10 megawatts are simply called "small." Considering that one megawatt provides enough electricity to power about 1,000 households, these small projects obviously could not be used to power a major city, but they are ideal for smaller communities.

*Not only is small-scale hydropower economical and green, it also brings communities together.*

The initial costs are also much lower than would be necessary to build a large dam.

While the power output of small-scale hydropower is low, the benefits to small communities can be great. Hydropower can be used to power machinery and replace muscle power. A project in Nepal used a simple turbine to power a corn grinder. This reduced labor time for flour preparation from 15 hours to 15 minutes. The extra time could be used by people to enhance their education or tend to other matters. A turbine and generator

can also produce electric light in areas where there was none before. With light comes better educational opportunities for people of that community. Small, remote towns in developed countries could use small-scale hydropower to meet their energy needs instead of hooking up to the power grid, which may be costly due to their location.

Developing countries are already seeing the benefits of these small projects. China, Latin America, and Southeast Asia are particularly promising markets. China's small-scale hydro projects already produce 20,000 megawatts, and plans are in place to install many more small-scale hydro projects over the next few years. Globally, small-scale hydro is expected to reach 55,000 megawatts by 2010. While these projects may seem best suited for the developing world, many communities in developed countries are also seeing the advantages of easy, virtually free energy. Not only is small-scale hydropower economical and green, it is also the type of project that brings communities together.

Other available forms of hydropower involve the oceans.

More than 70 percent of Earth's surface is covered with an ever-shifting body of water. Oceans have different densities, temperatures, pressures, and salt contents from top to bottom and from region to region. All of these natural features, as well as tides, waves, and marine currents, can be tapped for energy production. So far,

however, attempts to turn theory into practice have been disappointing, though recent developments in the United Kingdom and elsewhere may still prove otherwise.

There are several ways to harness the energy of the ocean. One way is to use the movement of tides to drive turbines. Such technology was used in the

**Small-scale hydro projects are a relatively inexpensive way to raise living standards in remote, underdeveloped communities.**

Middle Ages. "Tidal mills" worked by allowing the tides to fill a storage basin with water. In the basin was a wheel that was turned by the water entering and leaving. The waterwheels could

# GEOTHERMAL ENERGY

The sun has always been used for heat. Recently, scientists and engineers have begun using the variations in ocean temperatures at different depths to generate electricity. Earth makes its own heat as well. This energy, drawn from the hot rock and fluid within the Earth's crust, can be tapped to generate heat and electricity.

The upper 10 feet (3 m) of Earth is a consistent temperature of 50 to 60 °F (10–16 °C). Heat can be pumped up from the ground to heat and even cool buildings. The steam that rises from geothermal "mines"—geysers, springs, and underground reservoirs—can also be used to drive turbines that create electricity. Wells drilled 330 to 14,800 feet (100–4,500 m) below Earth's surface recover geothermal energy for commercial use. Some geothermal power plants use steam rising from reservoirs to power turbines and generators to produce electricity. Other geothermal plants might use the hot water to generate steam to power turbines.

In widespread use since the early 20th century, commercial geothermal energy has been on the increase since the 1970s. It now provides 9,000 megawatts of electricity and 9,000 megawatts for heating worldwide. Used in more than 45 countries, geothermal energy currently generates 10 to 20 percent of the electricity produced in Costa Rica, Kenya, and Nicaragua. In the United States, Alaska, Hawai'i, and the western states provide the best geothermal resources. Iceland and Greenland also make excellent use of their abundant geothermal resources.

Despite steady and significant growth, geothermal energy is not as green as other renewables. Though insignificant when compared to fossil fuels, geothermal energy does produce carbon dioxide emissions, and wells need to be drilled every few years. Also, some people do not even consider geothermal energy to be truly renewable since it cannot be replaced at the same rate it is used.

then be used to turn a grinding mill or similar form of machinery. In modern tidal barrages, a turbine attached to a generator replaces the waterwheel. The turbines are placed in a barrier that is built across a river estuary. Currently, there is only one commercially successful ocean project. It is France's tidal barrage at La Rance. Completed in 1967, it has an output of 240 megawatts, and is able to supply electricity for nearly three million people.

Though tidal barrages are a proven technology, high costs and environmental problems have prevented their widespread use. Marine life is disrupted during construction, which usually takes about 10 years. Disturbance of tides and currents is also damaging to local ecosystems. In addition, barrages only provide power for about 10 hours each day. Power during the remaining 14 hours must be provided by other methods. Finally, low output means most governments cannot justify the high financial and environmental costs.

Another possible alternative is wave power. Many different technologies have been designed to harness wave energy, but so far these have had little success. Rotating water columns or turbines suspended on floating buoys are examples of technologies being tried and improved. Great Britain currently has one operating wave farm, off the west coast of Scotland. It supplies power to a few hundred local homes. There are plans to develop a larger wave farm off the north coast of Scotland. Even though wave power would be environmentally friendly, so far it has proven too costly and inefficient to be considered an important source of energy.

Yet another possibility involving ocean hydropower is the utilization of the temperature difference between shallow and deep water to power turbines.

This complicated process is called ocean thermal energy conversion (OTEC). OTEC is now being developed by the government of Hawai'i. Fresh water is a byproduct of this process. It is hoped that this process may meet two needs—electricity and water.

There is no question that the ocean's energy potential is great. It is constantly moving, and it absorbs heat from the sun. This movement and heat can be used to produce energy, but because systems based on the ocean have a low efficiency, that energy is expensive. Even

though continued research and development may still result in clean, efficient, and inexpensive ocean-based energy, ocean power is expected to contribute only a tiny amount to world power in the near future.

## SCOTLAND'S STINGRAY

Though tidal barrages may not be the way of the future, other methods using tidal streams may still prove attractive. In September 2002, an offshore tidal generator, one of the world's first, was installed off the coast of Scotland's Shetland Islands. Sitting on the seabed within the tidal stream, this turbine is able to transform energy from the flowing water of the tidal stream into electricity. Capable of generating 150 kilowatts of electricity, the Stingray should be able to light hundreds of homes.

As a new technology, Stingray will be closely watched by scientists and developers. If successful, this **prototype** will pave the way for underwater tidal energy farms, which would use groups of turbines for increased energy output. Since such turbines would be submerged, it is thought that they would have minimal environmental and visual impact. With such a vast, predictable, high-energy resource—the ocean and its tidal streams—the availability of offshore tidal farms may well meet future demands for clean, renewable energy.

**The Stingray sits on the seabed between the islands of Bigga and Yell.**

## KEY CONCEPTS

**Estuaries** An estuary is a partially enclosed body of water where fresh water mixes with salty ocean water. Estuaries are found along coasts and are home to diverse ecosystems. Estuaries often act as traps for nutrients washed down toward the sea. This "soup" provides food and homes for various plants and animals, many of which are not found elsewhere. Major estuaries include San Francisco Bay, Puget Sound, Chesapeake Bay, Boston Harbor, and Tampa Bay.

**Turbines and generators** A water turbine is a circular, finned apparatus that is designed to convert the movement of flowing water into spinning energy. A generator can then use the spinning of the turbine to produce electricity. As long as the turbine spins, the generator produces electricity. Turbine designs are constantly being improved to reduce **friction** and convert more of the movement of water directly into electricity. When electricity is not needed, the power can be used to charge a battery. The energy stored in the battery can be used during periods of greater demand.

# Hydraulics Engineer

**Duties:** Designs dams and supervises construction
**Education:** Bachelor's degree in engineering
**Interests:** Construction, math, drawing, and physics

Navigate to the Environmental Careers Web site at **www.eco.org** for information about related careers. Also click on **www.engineeringjobs. com** for more information about jobs involving engineering.

# Careers in Focus

Hydraulics engineers are in charge of designing dams. They often organize and supervise construction, too. Although hydraulics engineers usually work on large-scale hydro projects, they can also design small-scale hydro projects.

Hydraulics engineers need to have strong math, drawing, and computer skills. They must also be familiar with building materials, environmental issues, and safety regulations. Analytical and problem-solving abilities should complement a keen eye for detail.

Most of the time, hydraulics engineers work in an office environment, where they use computer-aided design (CAD) systems to develop plans for the structure they are building. Occasionally, hydraulics engineers must visit job sites. When hydraulics engineers are conducting fieldwork, the conditions are often stressful. Surveying proposed dam sites may require travel to isolated areas, walking long distances on rocky terrain, working in confined spaces, and climbing to significant heights.

In order to succeed at their jobs, hydraulics engineers need to be creative, curious, analytical, and detail-oriented. They should be able to work as part of a team and communicate well, both orally and in writing. The ability to communicate clearly is important because much of a hydraulic engineer's work is becoming more diversified, and hydraulic engineers must interact with specialists in a wide range of fields outside engineering.

# Wind Energy's Potential

Not every location on the planet has access to running water to generate hydropower, but almost every place has wind. Humans have been using the power of wind for thousands of years. Windmills were a common sight across Europe and the Middle East for centuries. The wind's free energy was used to turn large millstones that ground staple foods such as corn into flour. Windmills were also used for pumping water to drain land. There was enough energy in wind to power huge sailing ships on their journeys across the oceans, but as coal, oil, and gas became increasingly available, these cheaper, more reliable energy sources overtook wind power. Coal and oil were used to generate electricity and made travel by boat more reliable. Windmills are now regaining popularity. Replace a millstone with a generator, and electricity is the result. Now, wind may again prove to be one of the world's most viable energy sources.

The Oil Crisis of the 1970s, along with growing concern for the environment, led to the development of modern wind

The vast, open plains of western Canada are ideal for wind farms. There are commercial wind farms in several sites in Alberta, Canada.

18

technology in the 1980s. Wind turbines, when well-situated, can produce electricity at costs that are competitive with fossil fuels. With a steady growth of 15 to 20 percent per year throughout the 1990s, it is no surprise that some experts estimate that wind power could eventually supply more than 30 percent of global electricity demand. In an effort to reduce carbon dioxide emissions, many countries have set targets for more wind energy production as part of a plan to increase the use of renewable energy resources. The countries making the most of wind power are Germany, the U.S., Denmark, Spain, and India.

India has huge energy demands that will only increase over time. The greenhouse gases produced as a result of burning fossil fuels affect not only India, but the

---

*Wind turbines can produce electricity at costs that are competitive with fossil fuels.*

---

rest of the world as well. Going green with wind power makes sense. As of October 2002, India had 1,702 megawatts of power coming from wind. The government sees the possibility of producing between 35,000 and 50,000 megawatts, but for now, they have set an ambitious target of 5,000 megawatts by 2012.

Like India, many countries in the developing world have huge wind resources that could be harnessed. These countries include Chile, Jordan, Morocco, and Pakistan. On a non-commercial scale, China makes excellent use of its wind by using it to pump water and charge electric batteries. China also uses wind to generate electricity in remote areas. Developing countries have the chance to avoid many of the ills associated with the use of fossil fuels, and some are beginning to do just that. Still, fossil fuels remain a very attractive option for poorer economies.

One of the greatest factors affecting whether or not wind

makes a big impact on world energy production is cost. For now and in the near future, wind energy will generally continue to cost more than fossil fuels. Still, as technology steadily improves and wind power generates a larger output, costs will decrease, bringing wind-power prices in line with oil and gas prices. Indeed, when external costs are taken into consideration, the price of wind power may already be in line with conventional energy sources.

Unlike fossil fuels, wind causes virtually no pollution. There are no solid or liquid wastes. There are no greenhouse gases. Even the production and disposal of equipment causes little in the way of pollution. Unlike nuclear power, which was once seen as the answer to the "power crisis," wind power is safe. It produces no toxic chemicals or other hazardous materials.

Wind is rarely in short supply. Deserts, great plains, coasts, and even the sides of freeways are good places for wind farms. Many of these places are remote and thinly populated, so wind farms are relatively non-disruptive. Also, there is no water necessary for cooling, as is the case with traditional generating stations. This means that wind power can be generated away from water sources.

Wind power is economically attractive to smaller companies. Producing more power simply requires more wind turbines.

Many governments are **privatizing** their energy industries in order to allow for competition and greater development. This lends itself to wind power. A wind farm can be constructed in a matter of months. Since a wind farm can be a much smaller project than a traditional power station, risks are more manageable. Even individuals can potentially buy a wind turbine. Wind farms can also improve rural economies, many of which have suffered as a result of increasing **urbanization**. Wind turbines can even be placed on existing farms and ranches, thus giving landowners an additional source of income.

One of the main problems with wind power is the initial cost. While the running costs are low, initial costs are huge. Finding and preparing a site

and buying and setting up all the equipment costs money. As well, wind turbines are still fairly rare. They will not be mass-produced until there is a very high demand for them. This keeps cost high. Private investors usually expect shorter payback periods, but paying off wind turbines takes a long time.

Another strike against wind power is that, unlike coal, oil, gas, and even wood, it cannot be stored for high-demand periods. Power is generated only when the wind is actually blowing. Though some excess power can be stored in batteries or pumped storage, for the most part it must either be wasted, used as it is created, or fed to an existing grid. Where continuous power is needed, wind installations may have to be backed up with other generating equipment using fossil fuels or hydro.

Wind turbines are constantly incurring the stresses of wind. Strong winds once cracked blades and shafts, but technology has since improved. Wind farms usually have 95 to 98 percent of their turbines working at any given time. Still, a tornado or severe storm could potentially destroy what amounts to an expensive investment. Noise created by turbines was once a major problem. It is also coming under control. Modern turbines are much quieter than those designed in the 1990s, and placement of turbines is often regulated. Poorly situated turbines can pose a danger to birds. However, this can be avoided by studying migration routes for local birds and avoiding those sites for future wind farms.

Though seemingly trivial, one of the most important problems associated with wind power is the appearance of the turbines themselves. While many find the turbines visually appealing, especially when compared to coal mines or power plants, others find them unsightly and do not want them "in their own backyard." In places such as Great Britain, there have been many protests against proposed wind farms. Some people feel that wind turbines interfere with scenic views and even tourism.

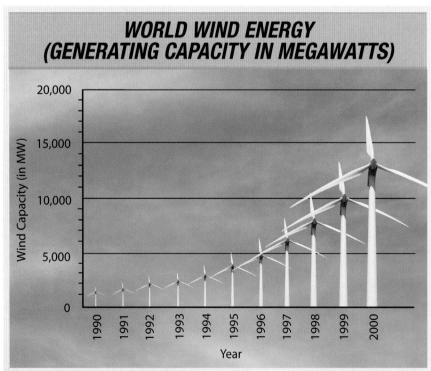

**WORLD WIND ENERGY (GENERATING CAPACITY IN MEGAWATTS)**

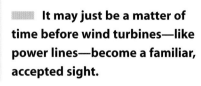

▨ **It may just be a matter of time before wind turbines—like power lines—become a familiar, accepted sight.**

# CARBON DIOXIDE EMISSIONS FROM POWER PLANTS

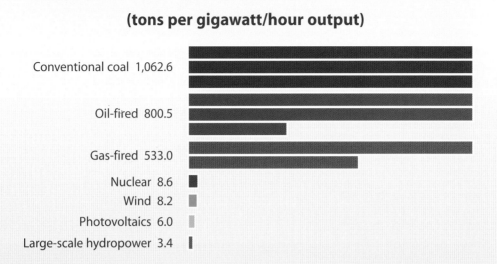

## (tons per gigawatt/hour output)

Conventional coal  1,062.6

Oil-fired  800.5

Gas-fired  533.0

Nuclear  8.6

Wind  8.2

Photovoltaics  6.0

Large-scale hydropower  3.4

Wind power is the third-cleanest form of energy production in large-scale use by humans. The amount of carbon dioxide produced from wind power is a fraction of that produced by traditional methods of making electricity.

## KEY CONCEPTS

**External costs** There are many costs associated with producing power that are not necessarily charged to customers. These costs include the atmospheric pollution that comes from processing plants and trucks that carry fuel supplies, as well as damage to landscapes caused by mining. Climate change and damage to human health are all costs that are not incurred in most forms of renewable energy. After external costs are factored in, renewable energy from wind, water, and the sun is often actually cheaper than traditional power.

**Oil Crisis** In 1973, Egypt and Syria attacked Israel in what is known as the Yom Kippur War.

The United States supported Israel with arms and equipment. This antagonized the members of the Organization of Petroleum Exporting Countries (OPEC), which included Iran, Kuwait, and Saudi Arabia. Saudi Arabia instituted an **embargo** on oil to the U.S. This embargo consisted of a price increase of nearly 200 percent. These events led to a great crisis for oil consumers. Lineups at gas stations were common, and President Nixon even tried to reduce the speed limit in the U.S. in order to conserve fuel. This crisis forced many people to begin thinking of alternative means of power, such as hydro, solar, and wind energy.

**Wind farms** Power is now being generated on a commercial scale in many places around the world at large installations called "wind farms." Wind farms consist of rows, or groupings of towers, typically 165 feet (50 m) high and sometimes even 300 feet (90 m) high. They are equipped with giant wind turbines for producing electricity. Denmark and Germany pioneered the development of commercial wind power, one of their fastest-growing industries. Commercial wind farms have also been established in Canada, India, Spain, and the United States. Many of the largest wind farms can be found in California, where some wind farms have thousands of turbines.

**Duties**: Researches, designs, constructs, and operates engines and machines
**Education**: Bachelor's degree in engineering
**Interests:** Math, science, and researching and designing new products

For information about a career in engineering, navigate to **www.bls.gov/oco/ocos027.htm** or check out **www.asee.org**

# Careers in Focus

A strong understanding of mathematics and scientific principles helps engineers develop new products. As well as researching and designing original concepts, engineers manufacture, test, and maintain products. There are many types of engineers, but it is primarily mechanical, electrical, and civil engineers who work with renewable energy resources.

Using computer-aided design (CAD), mechanical engineers research, develop, test, and maintain mechanical devices such as air-conditioning and refrigeration equipment. They research different forms of fuel and find new ways to make these sources available to users. They also supervise energy output sources such as power stations.

Electrical engineers also design, develop, and supervise the construction and maintenance of projects. These engineers specialize in the development of electrical devices, including electric motors, power stations, and equipment for generators. They find ways to improve existing energy sources and create more efficient means to produce power. Some electrical engineers specialize in power generation.

Civil engineers specialize in structural, water resources, environment, and geotechnical engineering. They determine construction needs and oversee the development of projects. Dams are one example of the type of project a civil engineer might oversee.

Mechanical engineers, electrical engineers, and civil engineers are all able to use their skills to help design and construct sources of renewable energy.

# Wind-Power Technology

There is a huge amount of energy in the wind. The key is to capture as much of it as possible. Wind turbines have changed in design throughout the years, from ancient wooden designs to modern ones built of steel. New designs are able to capture winds of lower speeds, with less energy wasted as friction, but the basic concepts behind turbine design have changed very little. Two or three blades make the rotor. The rotor is connected to the nacelle, which houses the generator and gearbox. The generator is where electricity is produced. The hub is the center point of the rotor, where all blades connect. The hub, generator, rotor, and blades all sit on top of a tubular tower. The amount of wind captured by a turbine is based on three factors: wind speed, rotor size, and air density.

## Wind Speed

The amount of energy in wind is found by cubing the wind's speed. For instance, if wind speed changes from 10 to 20 speed units, the energy in the wind changes from 1,000 to 8,000 energy units. This means that even a small increase in wind speed can turn into a large increase in power produced by a turbine. The operating range for turbines is between 13 and 65 feet (4–20 m) per second. A light breeze can power a turbine, but anything less is useless. Likewise, wind that is too strong can damage a wind turbine. This creates a need for a controller and a brake inside the hub.

**Engineers and wind-turbine manufacturers continually seek to improve wind-power technology.**

Average wind speeds depend on location. For instance, wind travels slowly at ground level because of friction with the ground. This is why turbine blades are now placed about 165 feet (50 m) above ground. Researchers are developing taller, larger turbines to take advantage of wind speeds high above the ground. Fast winds are found in coastal areas, on large bodies of water, and on open plains, where there is little to block them.

## Rotor Size

The amount of power produced changes with the area swept by the blades. The larger that area, the more power that can be produced. Large blades create problems, however. They put strain on the machinery of the hub, as well as the tower. Most rotors for wind pumps, which are used for smaller-scale energy production, are 6.5 to 23 feet (2–7 m) in diameter. Turbines used for commercial electricity generation have rotors between 65 and 130 feet (20–40 m) in diameter, though some are longer than 160 feet (50 m). Once again, as research and development continue, technology will improve. This should lead to larger rotors that create less strain on hub machinery, perhaps by using lighter materials.

*The basic concepts behind turbine design have changed little.*

## Air Density

Air gets thinner higher in the sky. Dense air has more energy in its movement than thinner air, so it is not usually efficient to place a turbine on a mountain or a high plateau. Turbines work better closer to sea level. In fact, offshore wind farms are an attractive idea for a couple of reasons. For one, they do not take up space on useful land.

## THE PARTS OF A WIND TURBINE

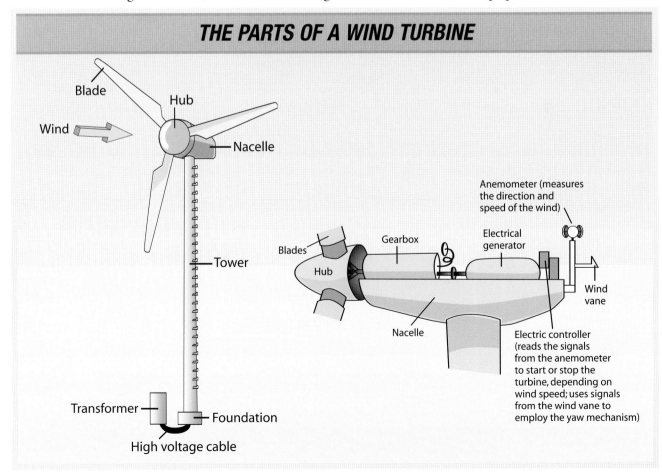

Blade
Hub
Wind
Nacelle
Tower
Transformer
Foundation
High voltage cable

Anemometer (measures the direction and speed of the wind)
Blades
Gearbox
Electrical generator
Hub
Nacelle
Wind vane
Electric controller (reads the signals from the anemometer to start or stop the turbine, depending on wind speed; uses signals from the wind vane to employ the yaw mechanism)

Old-fashioned windmills can still be seen throughout Europe. The Canary Islands of Spain have many examples of different types of windmills, some still in working order.

Second, there is less turbulence in the wind above water. Wind hitting projections on land such as hills and buildings creates turbulence. This turbulence can rock the blades of the turbine and cause stress and wear.

## THE BEAUFORT SCALE

Designed in the 19th century, the Beaufort scale is used to compare wind speeds. The scale ranges from 0 to 12, with 0 being absolute calm and 12 being hurricane-force winds. Wind speed is measured at 33 feet (10 m) above the ground. Modern wind turbines can operate between 3 (gentle breeze) and 10 (storms) on the Beaufort scale.

Turbine placement becomes a major issue when considering a wind-farm project. Placement can be difficult for many reasons. Wind speeds are not constant. They change every day. Also, the wind speed at one location may be quite different from a location even a short distance away. To determine a good site, detailed mathematical calculations are needed, but much data is required to make such calculations. Unfortunately, long-term wind speed data is difficult to obtain. A city may have sufficient data about wind speed, but wind farms are not built in cities. If there is no long-term data, there can be no calculations. Wind also changes from season to season and from year to year. There are even daily wind patterns to consider. These issues can make it difficult to determine a suitable site.

The science behind wind turbines includes much terminology from the field of aerodynamics. "Lift," "drag," "pitch," "yawing," and "furling" are all words that describe the laws of air. Knowing these laws allows scientists to maximize the power of wind. Knowledge of the science of wind has created a significant increase in the efficiency of wind turbines. In 1981, wind turbines averaged 50 kilowatts of power output. This increased to 160 kilowatts in 1990. Turbines with 600-kilowatt capacities are currently being produced.

Most new, commercial wind turbines have solid, tubular towers instead of lattice towers, such as those shown above. Lattice towers are thought to contribute to bird mortality, as they provide perches for birds.

## KEY CONCEPTS

### Furling, yawing, and pitch

"Furling" is a term used to refer to the shutting down of the rotor blades of a wind turbine when repair or maintenance is required. Furling is also necessary when wind speeds become too high. "Yawing" refers to a method of swiveling the rotor blades of a wind turbine to match changes in wind direction. On a pitch-controlled wind turbine, the turbine's electronic controller checks the power output of the turbine several times per second. When the power output becomes too high, it sends an order to the blade-pitch mechanism, which immediately pitches, or turns, the rotor blades slightly out of the wind. Conversely, the blades are turned back into the wind whenever the wind drops again.

# Mapping Renewable Energy Resources

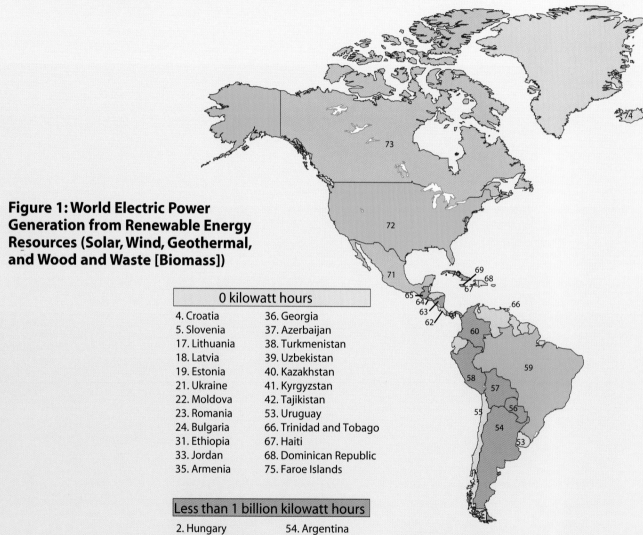

**Figure 1: World Electric Power Generation from Renewable Energy Resources (Solar, Wind, Geothermal, and Wood and Waste [Biomass])**

## 0 kilowatt hours

| | |
|---|---|
| 4. Croatia | 36. Georgia |
| 5. Slovenia | 37. Azerbaijan |
| 17. Lithuania | 38. Turkmenistan |
| 18. Latvia | 39. Uzbekistan |
| 19. Estonia | 40. Kazakhstan |
| 21. Ukraine | 41. Kyrgyzstan |
| 22. Moldova | 42. Tajikistan |
| 23. Romania | 53. Uruguay |
| 24. Bulgaria | 66. Trinidad and Tobago |
| 31. Ethiopia | 67. Haiti |
| 33. Jordan | 68. Dominican Republic |
| 35. Armenia | 75. Faroe Islands |

## Less than 1 billion kilowatt hours

| | |
|---|---|
| 2. Hungary | 54. Argentina |
| 3. Czech Republic | 56. Paraguay |
| 9. Luxembourg | 57. Bolivia |
| 13. Ireland | 58. Peru |
| 16. Poland | 60. Colombia |
| 20. Belarus | 61. Panama |
| 25. Greece | 63. Nicaragua |
| 28. Norway | 64. El Salvador |
| 32. Kenya | 65. Guatemala |
| 34. Turkey | 69. Jamaica |
| 52. South Korea | 70. Cuba |

## 1–5 billion kilowatt hours

| | |
|---|---|
| 1. Austria | 45. India |
| 6. Switzerland | 46. Thailand |
| 8. France | 47. Indonesia |
| 10. Belgium | 48. Australia |
| 11. Netherlands | 49. New Zealand |
| 27. Portugal | 55. Chile |
| 29. Sweden | 62. Costa Rica |
| 43. Russian Federation | 74. Iceland |
| 44. China | |

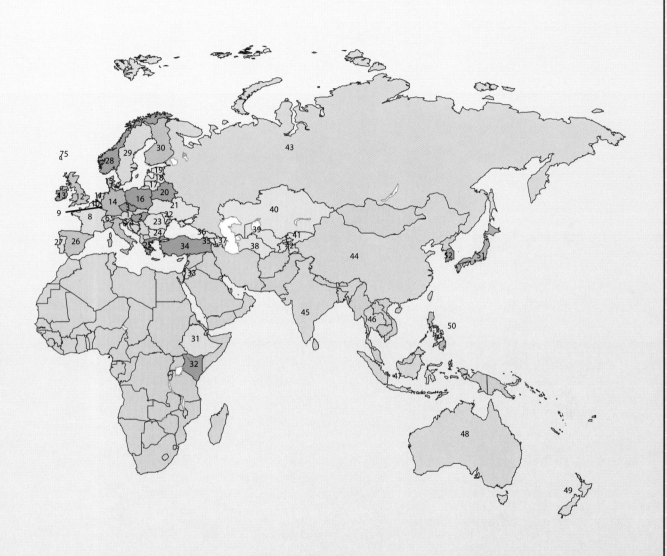

Scale 1:140,000,000

## 5–10 billion kilowatt hours

7. Italy
12. United Kingdom
15. Denmark
26. Spain
30. Finland
50. Philippines
71. Mexico
73. Canada

## 10–20 billion kilowatt hours

14. Germany
51. Japan
59. Brazil

## More than 20 billion kilowatt hours

72. U.S.A.

## No data available

# *Charting Renewable Energy*

**Figure 2:
World Total Primary
Energy Supply\* (2000)**

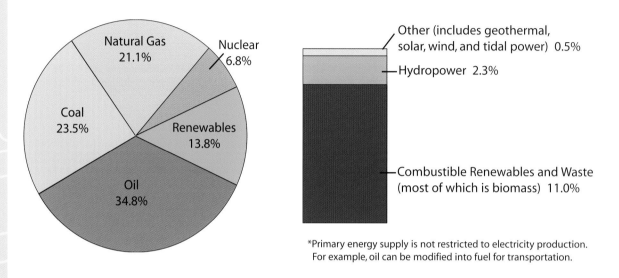

\*Primary energy supply is not restricted to electricity production.
For example, oil can be modified into fuel for transportation.

**Figure 3:
The Role of Renewables
in Electricity Production**

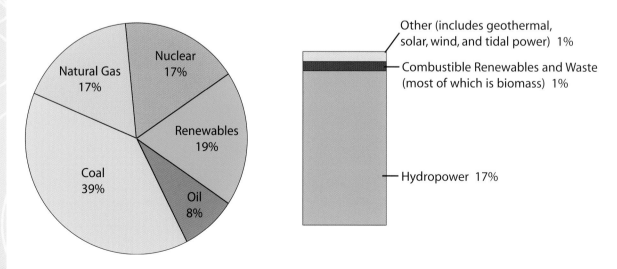

## Figure 4:
## Wind Energy: Installed Generating Capacity by Region (1999)

Africa 18 MW
Asia 1,437 MW
Europe 9,325 MW
Middle East 19 MW
North America 2,429 MW
Oceania 48 MW
South America 57 MW

## Figure 5:
## The Falling Cost of PV Energy

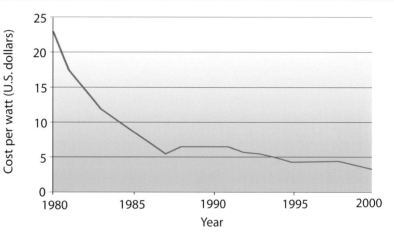

Cost per watt (U.S. dollars)

Year

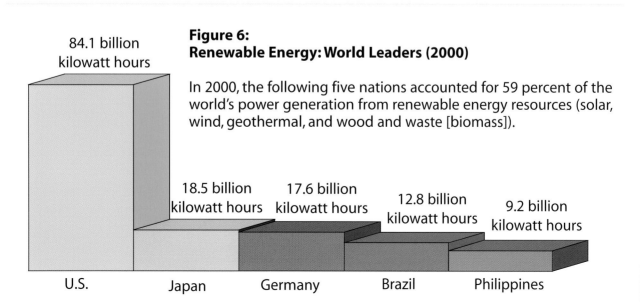

## Figure 6:
## Renewable Energy: World Leaders (2000)

In 2000, the following five nations accounted for 59 percent of the world's power generation from renewable energy resources (solar, wind, geothermal, and wood and waste [biomass]).

84.1 billion kilowatt hours

18.5 billion kilowatt hours

17.6 billion kilowatt hours

12.8 billion kilowatt hours

9.2 billion kilowatt hours

U.S.          Japan          Germany          Brazil          Philippines

# The Rebirth of Solar Power

Solar power is not a new idea. Early Greek and Roman builders knew how to create structures that took advantage of the sun's energy. Muslim architects built solar "chimneys" into their mosques, drawing hot air up from ground level and replacing it with cooler air from north-facing surfaces. In the 1880s, a solar-powered steam engine ran a printing press in France. In 1912, a solar-thermal installation in Cairo was running a 55-**horsepower** steam engine. But war destroyed the Cairo plant, while cheap oil and motor vehicles created a whole new industry. With the birth of this industry, there seemed to be no reason to bother with solar power anymore. Interest in solar energy did not reappear until the 1970s, when oil prices rose quickly and supplies were thought to be very limited. When prices fell in the 1980s, so did interest in solar power. Now, certain countries are once again taking advantage of the sun's energy.

Solar **radiation** can be used to warm or cool buildings, to provide hot water, and to

**This Stirling dish collector is just one of many types of devices that are being used to capture the thermal energy of the sun.**

generate steam for turbines producing electricity. Sunlight can be turned directly into electricity through photovoltaics,

*Solar energy is popular in areas that have high exposure to sunlight.*

a branch of solar science that is developing rapidly. Solar power fits into three main categories: passive solar, by which buildings are designed to take maximum advantage of the sun's radiation without the use of mechanical devices; solar thermal, which uses the sun's radiation to heat water systems and living spaces as well as generate electricity; and photovoltaics.

Solar-thermal energy, particularly as used for heating water and buildings, is a mature industry that is in widespread use in some countries. Most commonly used for domestic purposes, "low temperature" thermal systems are also used in industrial and agricultural processes. Like most forms of solar energy, solar thermal is especially popular in areas that have high exposure to sunlight. For example, one-third of the homes in Barbados have solar hot water heaters, and they are used in 90 percent of the buildings in Cyprus. It

is estimated that in subtropical climates, solar hot water systems can meet 80 to 100 percent of domestic hot water needs. In Europe, this number is between 50 and 65 percent. Many countries, such as Australia, Israel, and the Netherlands, have building regulations that encourage the use of solar collectors.

Solar collectors are used to harness the sun's thermal energy. Flat-plate collectors, which are generally used in domestic solar water heating systems, are the most common solar collector.

## SWITCH TO SOLAR

Following in the footsteps of Japan and Germany, the U.S. government is making an effort to encourage and increase the use of solar energy. In 2002, the Bush administration began working with the U.S. Congress and the solar energy industry to promote greater use of solar power as an alternative to fossil fuels. Accordingly, the Bush administration has proposed tax credits for adoption of solar energy technologies in homes. In addition, the United States Department of Energy (DOE) is working with the industry to reduce manufacturing costs and increase the power output of solar, or photovoltaic, cells.

Making use of the albedo effect, a flat black panel is used to absorb the sun's radiation. Pipes containing fluid are attached to the back of this panel, and the liquid is heated along with the panel. To prevent heat from escaping, the entire panel-tube system is encased in glass. The collector is normally placed on the roof, where it is best able to absorb the sun's energy. It is connected to a storage tank, where the hot water is stored until required. In commercial and industrial buildings, larger, more elaborate systems are used for heating water and space. Such systems include solar collectors, pumps, storage tanks, and heat exchangers.

The idea that solar collectors are only useful in hot climates is not true. There are more than 40,000 households with solar water in Great Britain, a place not known to have sunny skies.

In Scandinavia, solar water heating systems are being used for groups of homes. Solar hot water systems are now an established market, and a responsible choice for consumers.

The relatively new science of photovoltaics (PV) is proving to be the most exciting field in solar energy. PV modules power street lights in Zaire, water pumps in the Sudan, and small power stations in Germany, Italy, Japan, Spain, and the U.S. So far, the cost of PV electricity is generally much higher than that produced by fossil fuels and hydro. Still, PV is widely seen as one of the great emerging industries. The market is growing at about 20 percent a year. With technical improvements likely, costs are predicted to come down and demand is sure to grow.

The fuel for solar energy is free. Most equipment involved costs little to maintain. Solar power creates little or no pollution. It is easy to see why people are getting excited about solar science, but the big breakthroughs are yet to come. Researchers all over the world are trying to find ways to bring efficiency up and costs down. Without dedicated government support in countries around the world, it is likely to be many years before solar energy makes more than a small impact. The World Energy Council predicts that only three percent of total energy demand will be supplied by solar energy by 2020.

Still, enthusiasm for solar energy continues to grow. Berlin is the site of the newly completed International Solar Centre. The German parliament recently adopted the Renewable Energy Law (REL), which provides incentives for building owners who use PV for their buildings and for connection to the grid. In 1997, the Million Solar Roofs initiative was introduced in the United States as part of an effort to reduce greenhouse gas emissions.

Many governments know that solar power can reduce dependence on fossil fuels. By offering incentives, in the form of **subsidies**, grants, and tax breaks, for switching to renewable forms of energy, these governments will eventually be able to decrease spending on energy production.

## MILLION SOLAR ROOFS

On June 26, 1997, U.S. President Bill Clinton announced the Million Solar Roofs Initiative (MSRI), which is part of the United States' program to reduce greenhouse gas emissions. The aim is to install both PV and solar-thermal systems on one million rooftops across the U.S. by 2010. By working closely with the building industry, federal agencies, state governments, energy providers, and key businesses and organizations, the DOE hopes to strengthen the solar energy market. If all goes according to plan, carbon dioxide emissions could be reduced by the equivalent of the annual carbon dioxide emissions from 850,000 cars. MSRI could also create thousands of high-tech jobs and allow U.S. energy companies to remain competitive on a global scale, an important factor when one considers that by 2005, the PV market is expected to exceed $1.5 billion.

Solar-thermal systems can be used to heat swimming pools.

## KEY CONCEPTS

**Albedo effect** The albedo effect is the percentage of radiation reflected from a surface compared to the radiation striking it. Main factors affecting a rate of albedo are texture and color. Darker colors absorb more of the sun's rays, while lighter colors reflect the rays. A perfectly reflexive surface would have an albedo of 100. Earth has an albedo of about 30. Snow has a higher albedo than do grasslands or forests. When a rainforest is cleared, a higher albedo results.

**Sun** Earth's sun is a star about 93 million miles (150 million km) away. It generates heat and light in a continuous nuclear fusion reaction. Its core temperature is thought to be 27 million °F (15 million °C). Its power output is said to be 380,000,000,000,000,000,000 megawatts. Earth's surface receives about one kilowatt for every 10 square feet (1 sq m).

# Solar Applications

Instead of creating energy, passive solar saves it. In developed countries, almost one-third of the energy produced is used for heating, cooling, and lighting buildings. Passive solar systems can provide 60 to 70 percent of a building's energy needs with no carbon dioxide emissions. Unfortunately, most buildings we see around us were built at a time when fossil fuels were considered harmless. Windows are not strategically placed to best utilize the sun's energy, and buildings rely on electric power.

Solar architecture involves designing entire buildings to be giant collectors of solar energy. For example, in the Northern Hemisphere, sunlight is strongest on the southern faces of buildings. To take advantage of this, huge windows can be placed on the south-facing side of a building, while the north side is given minimal window area. Building materials for the walls, floors, and roofs of buildings can be selected for their ability to absorb and store heat. Roofs can become solar collectors. Even simple changes, such as planting deciduous trees around a building, can help. In the summer, the leaves block excessive sunlight and heat. In the winter, with the leaves gone, heat and light are allowed to reach the building.

Non-solar buildings that already exist cannot have their entire structures changed, but many other steps can be taken

to improve their energy efficiency. Improved insulation, better space heating, and the introduction of skylights are just some of the things that can reduce electricity costs while cutting down on carbon dioxide emissions. In some places, incentives are given to businesses that wish to install more efficient heating and cooling systems. There is much evidence to suggest that green buildings are not only cheaper to run, but more pleasant to work in. Companies based in green buildings experience greater productivity from their employees, with fewer sick days taken.

Developments in glass, insulation, and architectural design are leading to buildings that use much less electricity for

---

*Evidence suggests that green buildings are not only cheaper to run, but more pleasant to work in.*

---

heat, light, and cooling. With the addition of photovoltaics, such buildings can become truly self-sufficient. PV modules and arrays can be added to roofs and facades. In new buildings, PV can even be integrated directly into windows, tiles, and roof shingles. Considering that office buildings use most of their electricity during the day, solar power—produced only during daytime hours—could be the ultimate solution for commercial

**Solar One was the world's first major solar plant. A demonstration project, it highlighted the potential and drawbacks of industrial solar-thermal power.**

power usage. Since buildings consume so much energy in the developed world, solar architecture could help in the fight against global warming. It could also help conserve fossil fuels for future use.

Unlike passive solar, which seeks to save the sun's energy, solar power plants are an attempt to turn solar energy into a large-scale producer of electricity. Like traditional power plants, the idea is to generate steam to turn turbines. In the case of solar-thermal plants, sunlight, not fossil fuel, is the fuel used to generate steam.

Industrial, or high-temperature, solar-thermal systems use concentrating collectors to help harness solar power. This can involve one of three systems. One method uses mirrored troughs with a tube of fluid, usually oil, running above and along their length. Sunlight is reflected and focused on the fluid, which runs back to a storage tank. Later, it produces steam, which is used to generate electricity.

## SMART GLASS

Many companies are now producing glass that takes advantage of sunlight. This specially coated glass lets in short-wave radiation—sunlight—but prevents long-wave radiation—heat—from escaping. This glass actually acts as insulation, helping buildings retain heat that would be lost through regular glass. Coating existing windows with a special film achieves similar results. Some coatings will even darken as the sun gets too intense. Transparent insulation, which can take the form of glass bricks or building blocks, allows light in while retaining heat.

A second method uses a large array of mirrors, called heliostats, which rotate with the sun and reflect light to a receiving tower. Again, a fluid is heated and runs down the tower to eventually produce steam. The final method uses parabolic dishes to collect sunlight to power Stirling engines. In each method, large reflective surfaces are used to focus light on a desired location. As in traditional forms of power generation, electricity is produced indirectly. Steam generation and turbine-turning are the steps that produce energy. These stations may need a backup of traditional power to produce electricity for nighttime hours. Such stations are referred to as hybrids.

So far, such plants have had only limited success. Though solar power stations operate in the U.S. and Australia, and development is underway in places such as Kuwait, Mexico, South Africa, and Switzerland, it is difficult to tell whether industrial solar thermal has a serious future in world energy production. Output does not compare well with traditional power plants. Many fossil fuel plants produce 1,000 megawatts or more, while even the largest solar plants only produce 350 megawatts. Though in theory the sun has tremendous energy potential, it is extremely difficult to collect on such a large scale.

Climate change has also made governments and investors nervous about putting money into large-scale projects that depend so heavily on the weather. Shifting weather patterns could make expensive plants useless one day. Despite some successes, solar thermal still needs more research and development before it becomes a major source of electricity.

## SOLAR ONE AND SOLAR TWO

The world's first major solar power plant was built in the Mojave Desert in California. Completed in 1982, Solar One used a large group of heliostats and a receiving tower to produce 10 megawatts of electricity for the grid. A follow-up plant, called Solar Two, was built between 1996 and 1998. It operated a similar system, but it used molten salt rather than water as a "receiving fluid." The hot salt could be stored for days before being used to heat the water that drove the turbine that generated electricity. This meant that the sun's energy could be used even at night or in cloudy conditions. Solar Two, in particular, was a great success. Like Solar One, it produced 10 megawatts of electricity, enough to power 10,000 households, but it was even more reliable. Despite this success, Solar Two has been converted into a tool used by astronomers to study outer space.

## KEY CONCEPTS

**Concentrating collectors**
Concentrating collectors focus dispersed light to a point, usually by using curved mirrors or parabolic dishes. The idea is to focus as much light as possible on the liquid to be heated in order to produce the steam that turns the turbine. Curved mirrors can reflect a great deal of light on one spot, creating intense heat. The two most common types of collectors are parabolic troughs and parabolic dishes. The focal point should be made of a material that absorbs heat very well.

**Stirling engine** A Stirling engine uses heat to produce motion. In that way, it is like a turbine generator, only smaller. The gas inside the engine is sealed in and drives a piston as it is heated. Stirling engines operate equally well on multiple types of fuel, such as natural gas, propane, alcohol, hydrogen, gasoline, diesel or bio-diesel, or heat from the sun. Since nothing is combusted inside a Stirling engine, it produces no waste exhaust. If sunlight is used to provide the heat that drives the engine, there is no pollution involved at all.

# Architect

**Duties**: Conceives, advises, and draws designs for homes and other buildings
**Education**: Bachelor of Arts degree in architecture
**Interests**: Designing, planning, buildings, and art

Navigate to the Web site **www.archfoundation.org/** for more information about a career in architecture. Also click on **www.careers.iptv.org/enhanced/1139/ec_careerhome.cfm** for detailed information about life as an architect.

# Careers in Focus

The construction of every building takes months, even years, of careful planning, model-making, and compromise. Architects are the masterminds behind these projects, organizing and overseeing the development of huge condominium complexes, concert halls, tiny country cottages, and wheelchair-accessible homes.

Developers, home owners, and companies hire architects to create design ideas and then plan and develop these designs. After analyzing clients' requests, architects meet regularly with their clients to consult on the styles, features, colors, and materials to be used. They must also be aware of local legislation concerning building requirements and restrictions and apply for relevant permits. Before the building's foundation can be laid,

the architect must make sketches and models for the clients so that they can have a clear understanding of the design. They also provide blueprints for contractors and construction workers. Architects must also ensure that the project stays within time and financial budgets.

Architects must acquire a university education before they are able to practice in the field. While most universities do not require prerequisite courses for entry into architectural programs, it is useful to have knowledge of design, computers, graphics, history, geography, math, physics, and art. After completing an architecture program, it is important to take additional courses to become familiar with new technology.

# The Photovoltaic Revolution

In 1839, the French physicist Antoine Henri Becquerel discovered that a small amount of electricity was produced when light fell on certain materials. This meant that electricity could be produced directly from the sun, with no need for steam and turbines. By the 1890s, this discovery was already fueling the dream of pollution-free energy. Such dreams were premature, however. Early attempts to produce electricity from sunlight only succeeded in converting one percent of incoming light to electricity. With oil being cheap and plentiful, large-scale development of solar technology was put on hold and a "century of smoke" was to follow. Now the dream of pollution-free energy may finally be close to being realized.

Photovoltaics is widely considered the most promising aspect of solar energy, and perhaps of all renewables. Converting electricity directly from sunlight, solar cells cause little pollution, no noise, and no emissions. Long-lasting and low

**This PV installation, in Lausanne, Switzerland, provides electricity to the city's trolley-bus lines.**

maintenance, they work well even in cloudy conditions. They can be integrated into building designs and connected to grids.

*PV is widely considered the most promising aspect of solar energy, and perhaps of all renewables.*

They are especially useful in remote areas and in places where conventional power is too expensive, unreliable, or simply nonexistent.

Despite PV's potential, drawbacks remain. Getting cost-effective energy from the sun is a major challenge. Even with the latest, much-improved solar cells, PV electricity still costs 4 to 10 times as much as energy produced by fossil fuels, though prices are beginning to come down. What keeps costs high is the issue of energy conversion. How much of the sunlight going into a PV can be turned into useable energy? The technology is steadily improving, however. In 1954, a solar cell that could convert six percent of light into electricity had been developed. By the late 1980s, conversion efficiency was up to 15 percent

in laboratory settings. Cells with conversion rates higher than 30 percent are now available. While this does not sound like much, consider that combustion engines, such as those in a car, achieve only 20 to 25 percent conversion. Fossil fuel power plants convert coal to electricity at a rate of 30 to 35 percent, but with serious consequences for the environment.

Though many different types of PV technology are currently under development, there are three main types of solar cells being commercially produced. The most efficient tend to be monocrystalline, or single crystal, solar cells. They are made with silicon, which is cheap and plentiful. Silicon crystal is the same material used in computer chips, and solar cells require the same precise construction in order to be useful. Polycrystalline solar cells are made from lower-quality silicon. Though this type of solar cell is less efficient, it is cheaper to produce. Many consider thin-film solar cells to be the most promising. In this type of solar cell, a semiconductor material is deposited on material such as glass or aluminum in a process that is similar to tinting glass.

Although they are generally half as efficient as monocrystalline and polycrystalline cells, thin-film cells are also far cheaper to produce and, as a result, are widely used.

Whatever its design, a PV cell can only produce a fraction of a volt of power. Because light spreads out, huge panels of PV cells are needed before a significant amount of electricity can be produced. PV cells are not useless, however. They can be used to provide energy for anything from watches and calculators to homes, large buildings, and for industrial purposes. Every building has flat surfaces that could hold PV panels without using extra space. PV systems can be used in combination with other technologies to provide energy for the grid. There are even some PV power plants in existence, a number of which are found in the U.S. Even the Pentagon now uses a PV system for power.

Sales of PV cells have grown steadily every year. In 1970, there were virtually no PVs available. By 1995, solar cells were producing 120 megawatts worldwide. Still, the technology available is not efficient enough to warrant the construction of many major, large-scale power plants. The White Bluff Solar Station in Richland, Washington, began operation in May 2002 and is the largest solar PV plant in the Pacific Northwest. It is expected to produce about 30 kilowatts of power. The construction cost of $230,000 was aided by programs of the DOE. Supporters of this type of project foresee the coming of 100-megawatt super stations and an end to the smokestacks of the past century.

On its own or when combined with other forms of energy, PV is a useful and flexible technology. PV "power plants" can be built almost anywhere, on existing rooftops and along freeways rather than in large, central arrays that take up vast amounts of land, as do solar-thermal plants and conventional power plants. PV is also flexible in that it can be used and combined with other energy systems, including wind and hydropower. In order to generate more power, the simple addition of more PV panels is all that is

**This PV/diesel-hybrid power system was built to provide electricity to the 45 residents of a remote Alaskan village.**

## A SOLAR HYDROGEN FUTURE?

Perhaps of greatest interest is the role that PV is likely to play in what some are calling the "hydrogen economy" of the distant future. One of the most common elements on Earth, hydrogen will never run out. The problem is that it exists only in compounds such as water ($H_2O$), from which it must be separated in order to be used as a fuel. To do this, fossil fuels, or other expensive and polluting forms of electricity, are commonly used. Though the end result—hydrogen as fuel—is pollution-free and in fact releases only water, it remains expensive, both in terms of actual and external costs. Many believe that the cleaner, more efficient solar cells used to produce hydrogen will make hydrogen-powered cars and buildings a reality. Hydrogen could also become an energy carrier, storing and delivering energy to consumers.

required. Much time and money has been invested in this promising branch of solar energy, and so PV technology is expected to continue to improve rapidly.

Renewable energy offers clean alternatives to fossil fuels. More flexible and small-scale than traditional, centralized operations, renewables work well for remote areas and smaller communities, bringing energy and its benefits to places where it is much needed. Being smaller, renewable systems can be tailored to local needs. Plus, renewable energy resources are limitless. Today, governments and energy companies are beginning to show an interest in wind, water, and solar power, and a shift to renewables seems inevitable. Until costs come down, and as long as oil and gas reserves last, renewables may not be given the attention they deserve.

## BIOENERGY

While photovoltaics is one of the newest major forms of renewable energy, bioenergy is one of the oldest. Biomass, which refers to any plant or animal matter, can be used to provide bioenergy in the form of heat, fuel, and electricity. Unlike coal, oil, and gas, which are being used much faster than they can form, biomass can be continuously renewed. Wood, in particular, has been a mainstay for heating for thousands of years.

Technology now allows us to use biomass in new ways to produce heat and even electricity. Agricultural, animal, and even municipal wastes can all be used to generate energy. Byproducts from logging and the pulp and paper industry are also used. "Energy crops" such as corn are often specifically grown to provide various forms of bioenergy. Sugarcane is another particularly useful energy crop.

Biomass can be used in power plants, where it can be burned to produce steam and power turbines. It can also be converted into liquid fuel, which can be used to power cars and even industrial operations. Despite its versatility, drawbacks remain. Energy crops may use precious land. The burning of biomass still produces carbon dioxide emissions, though in lesser quantities than fossil fuels. In addition, the energy output from biomass is still comparatively small.

Solar cells have long been popular in developing countries. PV systems as small as 3.28 square feet (1 sq m) are able to produce between 20 and 100 watts of electricity, enough to meet a household's needs.

## KEY CONCEPTS

**Energy conversion** Energy comes in many forms, including light, heat, sound, electricity, energy of movement, and chemical energy. Energy can be converted or changed from one form to another. For instance, when gasoline burns in the engine of a car, it converts from chemical energy to the energy of motion, as well as heat. Similarly, the energy of wind's movement can be turned into electricity. Electricity can be converted into sound in a stereo. Most types of power plants use heat to boil water and turn turbines, which then produce electricity. Many energy conversions, however, produce waste heat that cannot be used.

**Photovoltaic (PV) cells** The word "photo" means "light," and "voltaic" means "electric." Commonly called solar cells, PV cells are made of special materials called semiconductors, such as silicon. When light strikes the cell, a certain portion of it is absorbed within the semiconductor material. This allows the energy of the absorbed light to be transferred to the semiconductor.

The energy knocks electrons loose, allowing them to flow freely. By attaching metal contacts to each cell, these electrons can be drawn away, creating a "current" that will power anything from lights to washing machines. Connecting many of these cells together results in solar modules or panels. Modules can be interconnected to form arrays. About 10 to 20 arrays usually provide enough power for the average household. For industrial and electric utility applications, hundreds of arrays are interconnected.

**Born**: February 18, 1745, in Como, Italy
**Died**: March 5, 1827
**Legacy**: Invented the electric battery. The "volt" is named after Volta.

Navigate to the Web site **www.ideafinder.com/history/ inventors/volat.htm** to learn more about Alessandro Volta. Also click on **http://ppp.unipv.it/Volta** for more information about Volta.

# People in Focus

Alessandro Volta was an Italian physicist known for his work with electricity. Born in Como, Italy, he was educated in public schools. Although he did not speak until the age of four, he soon caught up with and exceeded his peers. By the age of 14, he had already decided to become a physicist. In 1774, he became a professor of physics at the Royal School in Como. The next year, he invented the electrophorus, an instrument that produced charges of static electricity. This earned him a great deal of fame. In 1799, Volta began teaching at the University of Pavia, also in Italy. He taught there for 25 years.

Though he had already achieved a certain amount of fame for his scientific work, it was not until 1800 that Volta truly made a place for himself in history by developing a device that produced a large and steady flow of electricity. Called the voltaic pile, Volta's device was essentially the first ever electric battery.

Volta received many awards for this revolutionary invention. In 1801, Volta presented his battery to the Institut de France, in the presence of First Consul Napoleon, who honored him with the gold medal. In 1809, when Napoleon became Emperor, he appointed Volta a senator of the newly constituted Kingdom of Italy and gave him the title of count in 1810. Perhaps the greatest honor bestowed on Volta, however, was the naming of the electrical unit the "volt" after him.

# Time Line of Events

**circa 6000 B.C.**

A magnifying glass is used to concentrate the sun's rays to make fire.

**5000 B.C.**

Wind energy propels boats along the Nile River in Egypt.

**circa 2000 B.C.**

Greeks and Romans use "burning mirrors" as weapons of war by focusing sunlight to ignite fires and burn the sails of enemy warships.

**200 B.C.**

Windmills are used to pump water in China and grind grain in Persia and the Middle East.

**100 B.C.**

Greeks use water to turn wheels for grinding wheat into flour.

**A.D. 100**

Italian historian Pliny the Younger builds a passive solar home. He uses glass to keep heat in and cold out.

**1000s**

Windmills are used extensively for food production in the Middle East. Returning merchants and crusaders carry this idea back to Europe.

**1300s**

Anasazi people in North America live in south-facing cliff dwellings that capture the winter sun.

**1767**

Swiss scientist Horace de Saussure invents the first solar collector in the form of a solar hot box.

**1800s**

U.S. settlers use windmills to pump water for farms and ranches and, later, to generate electricity for homes and industry.

**1870s**

Augustin Mouchot, a French mathematics teacher, uses solar cookers, solar water pumps for irrigation, and solar stills for wine and water distillation.

**1881**

Niagara Falls lights city street lamps.

**1940**

Approximately 40 percent of electrical generation in the U.S. is from hydropower. This drops to about 10 percent by 2000.

**1941**

Approximately 60,000 solar water heaters are in use in Florida.

**1954**

Solar cells are invented.

**1973**

The Organization of Petroleum Exporting Countries (OPEC) imposes the first oil embargo. OPEC stops selling oil to the U.S. and increases the price of oil by 70 percent to the United States' European allies.

**1977**

The Alliance to Save Energy is founded, and the DOE is created. President Jimmy Carter creates a new federal department to coordinate energy policy and programs. Energy efficiency and renewable energy programs receive major funding. Carter installs solar panels on the White House and promotes incentives for solar energy systems.

**Despite continuing improvements in solar and wind technology, hydropower will likely remain the leader in renewable energy resources well into the future.**

**1978**

Automobile fuel economy standards take effect, resulting in a doubling of the average new car's fuel efficiency. This saves the United States 2.5 million barrels of oil per day.

**1979**

The Iranian revolution generates the second world oil crisis, doubling oil prices and plummeting the industrial world into a recession. The Three Mile Island accident puts a stop to new orders for U.S. nuclear power plants.

**1986**

Chernobyl, in the Ukraine, is the site of the most devastating nuclear accident in history, renewing global interest in energy efficiency.

**1993**

President Bill Clinton proposes a small tax that would encourage people to invest in energy efficiency, but Congress rejects his proposal.

**1995**

The Intergovernmental Panel on Climate Change announces that "the balance of evidence suggests a discernible human influence on global climate."

**1997**

The Kyoto Conference on Global Climate Change draws international attention to the global warming issue and the connection to fossil fuels.

**1999**

President Clinton calls for the federal government to reduce its energy use by 2010 to 35 percent of the 1985 levels. He also calls for the government to cut its greenhouse gas emissions to 30 percent below the 1990 levels.

**2001**

Under President George W. Bush, the U.S. decides not to participate in the Kyoto Protocol.

**2002**

The Earth Summit takes place in Johannesburg, South Africa.

# Concept Web

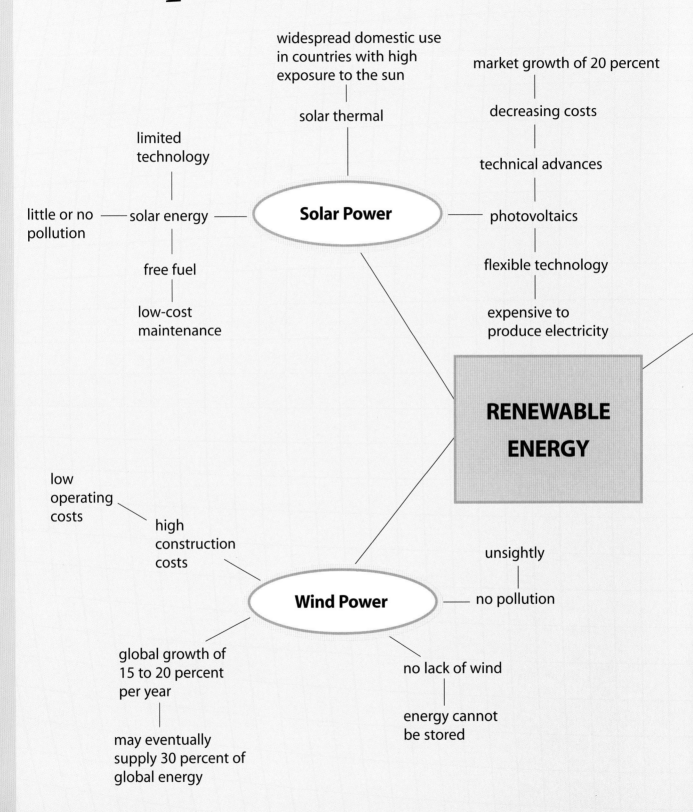

widespread domestic use in countries with high exposure to the sun

solar thermal

market growth of 20 percent

decreasing costs

limited technology

technical advances

little or no pollution — solar energy — **Solar Power** — photovoltaics

free fuel

flexible technology

low-cost maintenance

expensive to produce electricity

**RENEWABLE ENERGY**

low operating costs

high construction costs

unsightly

**Wind Power** — no pollution

global growth of 15 to 20 percent per year

no lack of wind

may eventually supply 30 percent of global energy

energy cannot be stored

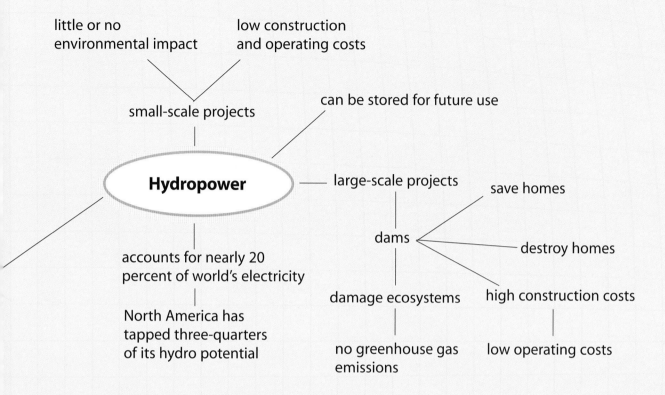

## MAKE YOUR OWN CONCEPT WEB

A concept web is a useful summary tool. It can also be used to plan your research or help you write an essay or report. To make your own concept web, follow the steps below:

- You will need a large piece of unlined paper and a pencil.
- First, read through your source material, such as *Renewable Energy Resources* in the Understanding Global Issues series.
- Write the main idea, or concept, in large letters in the center of the page.
- On a sheet of lined paper, jot down all words, phrases, or lists that you know are connected with the concept. Try to do this from memory.
- Look at your list. Can you group your words and phrases in certain topics or themes? Connect the different topics with lines to the center or to other "branches."
- Critique your concept web. Ask questions about the material on your concept web: Does it all make sense? Are all the links shown? Could there be other ways of looking at it? Is anything missing?
- What more do you need to find out? Develop questions for those areas you are still unsure about or where information is missing. Use these questions as a basis for further research.

# Quiz

## Multiple Choice

1. Which form of solar energy does not involve the production of electricity?
   a) solar thermal
   b) solar architecture
   c) photovoltaics
   d) active solar

2. Which is the biggest unit in this list?
   a) megawatt (MW)
   b) terawatt (TW)
   c) gigawatt (GW)
   d) kilowatt (KW)

3. America's largest proportion of renewable energy comes from:
   a) solar power
   b) hydropower
   c) wind power
   d) nuclear power

4. Presently, most of the world's energy comes from:
   a) nuclear
   b) natural gas
   c) hydro
   d) oil and coal

5. Which form of renewable energy can be useful at all levels of operation, from large power plants to small community or individual operations?
   a) solar
   b) wind
   c) water
   d) all of the above

## True or False

1. Wind power is only useful at relatively high wind speeds.
2. In the U.S., more energy comes from hydro than from wind.
3. "Solar power" includes the heating of water for households.
4. Global warming may change weather patterns.
5. Nuclear power is a renewable form of energy.

## Where Did It Happen?

1. Building of the largest producer of hydroelectric power in the U.S.
2. Construction of the Three Gorges Dam.
3. Development of the world's only commercially successful ocean power project.
4. The first major solar power plant built in the U.S.
5. One of the countries that has a major wind farm.

**Answers on page 53**

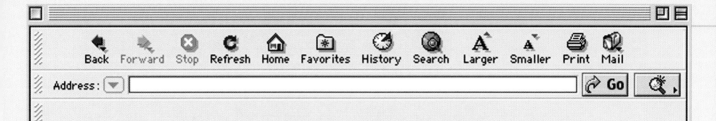

# *Internet Resources*

**The following Web sites provide more information on renewable energy:**

## United Nations Environment Programme, Energy and OzonAction Branch
http://www.uneptie.org/energy

This Web site is an excellent source of information on energy-related issues around the world. From climate change and other environmental consequences to energy use and policy, this site offers information on all the regions of the world. Reader-friendly fact sheets on the various types of renewable energy resources allow for quick overviews of the various technologies available.

## U.S. Department of Energy, Office of Energy Efficiency and Renewable Energy
http://www.eren.doe.gov

From fact sheets to careers and national and international news on renewable energy, this DOE Web site provides all the information you need to learn more about renewables in the U.S. Links to various associations, tips on energy efficiency, and "Ask an Energy Expert" are all useful and interesting features.

**Some Web sites stay current longer than others. To find other renewable energy Web sites, enter terms such as "renewable energy," "alternative energy," or "sustainable energy" into a search engine.**

# Further Reading

Berinstein, Paula. *Alternative Energy: Facts, Statistics, and Issues.* Westport, CT: Oryx Press, 2001.

Geller, Howard S. *Energy Revolution: Policies for a Sustainable Future.* Washington, D.C.: Island Press, 2003.

Hawkes, Nigel. *New Energy Sources (Saving Our World).* Brookfield, CT: Copper Beech Books, 2000.

Riley, Dohn. *Turning the Corner: Energy Solutions for the 21st Century.* Tahoe City, CA: Alternative Energy Institute, 2001.

Scheer, Hermann. *Solar Economy: Renewable Energy for a Sustainable Global Future.* Sterling, VA: Earthscan, 2002.

Walisiewicz, Marek. *Alternative Energy.* New York: DK Publications, 2002.

*Answers*

**Multiple Choice**
  1. b)   2. b)   3. b)   4. d)   5. d)

**True or False**
  1. F   2. T   3. T   4. T   5. F

**Where Did It Happen?**
  1. Grand Coulee Dam   2. China   3. La Rance, France   4. Mojave Desert, California
  5. Canada, Denmark, Germany, India, Spain, U.S.

# Glossary

**bioenergy:** the use of organic matter to produce electricity, heat, fuels, and chemicals

**commercial:** capable of producing a profit

**developed countries:** countries in the industrialized world; highly economically and technologically developed

**developing world:** the countries in the world that are undergoing the process of industrialization

**ecosystems:** systems formed by the interaction of plants and animals with the environment

**embargo:** restriction placed on commercial activity; enforced by law

**fossil fuels:** carbon-containing fuels, such as coal, oil, and natural gas, that are derived from the decomposed remains of prehistoric organisms

**friction:** the force that resists motion between two bodies that are in contact

**geothermal:** relating to the heat of Earth's interior

**green:** advocating or promoting environmentalism; environmentally sound or beneficial

**horsepower:** a unit of power equivalent to 745.7 watts

**Industrial Revolution:** the change from an agricultural to an industrial society, which began in England in the mid-18th century and is continuing in some countries today

**organic:** derived from plants or animals

**photovoltaics:** a field of technology involving the direct conversion of sunlight into electricity

**privatizing:** transferring public property and services from public or government control to private control

**prototype:** the original model for a system, device etc.

**radiation:** the process in which energy is emitted as particles or waves (from the sun)

**renewable energy:** energy resources that are natural and potentially endless

**reservoir:** a natural or artificial place where water is collected and stored for use

**subsidies:** financial aid given by the government to an individual, company, or another government

**turbine:** a rotary device used in hydro and wind power. The design differs for each use, but generally, their turning is enough to crank a generator and produce electricity

**urbanization:** a population shift from rural to urban areas

# Index

# Photo Credits